HIDDEN L~~~~

an artist's eye for detail

Marietta Van Dyck

To Paul and Angela

Copyright © Marietta Van Dyck, 1998

Cover illustration: Courtyard of the Star Gallery, Castle Ditch Lane. The courtyard at the side of the Star Gallery and workshops is hidden away between Fisher Street (approached by a narrow covered alleyway) and the cul-de-sac known as Castle Ditch Lane. The conversion of the former Beards Brewery and adjoining buildings has been carried out in a sympathetic manner with an interesting mix of old and new tile, brick and flint. Some of the details over the rooftops include a terracotta finial, a stone ball above the Assembly Rooms and small brick arches on the chimneys.

Title page illustration: Carved wooden bee, South Street (not on map). This low relief carving of a bee on the front of a window box is an amusing little detail which deserves repainting and varnishing.

ISBN 0 9519876 9 0
British Library Cataloguing-in-Publication Data.
A catalogue record of this book is available from the British Library.

Published by Pomegranate Press, Church Cottage, Westmeston, Sussex BN6 8RH

Printed by Ghyllprint Ltd, The Ghyll Print Centre, Heathfield, East Sussex TN21 8AW Tel: 01435 8662

Introduction

*I*n 1904 E.V. Lucas, the author of *Highways and Byways in Sussex*, after visiting the town wrote: 'Lewes is the museum of Sussex; for she has managed to compress into a small compass more objects of antiquarian interest than any other town I know.'

A relative newcomer to Lewes, I moved here with my family in 1990. While exploring the streets and the twittens in Lewes, Cliffe and Southover I gradually built up my collections of photographs of both well known and lesser known views, in particular the many and diverse architectural details. I have come to love this ancient and attractive town which has afforded the inspiration and opportunity to make nearly one hundred detailed pen and ink drawings, a selection of which is featured in this book.

The interesting and unusual subjects which I have come across continue to surprise and delight me. With one or two exceptions the details I have illustrated here are not physically obscured from view. They are, however, largely hidden from the casual or unobservant person. My aim is to encourage readers to search out and enjoy these details, which will often be found well above eye level.

Friends and acquaintances continue to suggest new subjects for my drawings which I have not yet discovered. In this book I have attempted to give a flavour of hidden Lewes but, because of constraints of space, a number of drawings are not featured. Those of you who are interested and observant, whether as resident or visitor, will no doubt enjoy spotting other details. Sadly, some of the objects I have recorded have disappeared, and I mourn these losses since they all form an integral part of the charm and appeal which Lewes holds for many.

I hope that my drawings capture some of the essential qualities so many of us take for granted, and will encourage all who love Lewes to preserve as many of these public treasures as possible for the benefit of future generations. Who knows: perhaps Lewes people will be inspired to add new, unique and finely crafted details to their private and public buildings.

Marietta Van Dyck

Acknowledgements:

I am grateful to Fran Whittle,co-ordinator of *Lewes News*, for encouraging me to contribute an 'Eye for Detail' drawing for each issue since November 1991. Many of the drawings in this book first appeared there.

Long time residents of Lewes have been very helpful with historical and technical information, and particular thanks go to the respected historians Dr Colin Brent and Mrs Judith Brent, who kindly checked my captions before publication.

John Hollands provided useful information about the railways and the Wyvern finial: my thanks for his help.

Select bibliography:

Colin Brent, *Georgian Lewes*, Colin Brent Books 1993
Colin Brent, *Historic Lewes*, Lewes Town Council 1993
Alec Clifton Taylor, *Six More English Towns*, BBC 1981
Brigid Chapman, *The Weathervanes of Sussex*, Temple House Books 1987
Edna & Mac McCarthy, *History Trail of Lewes*, S.B. Publications
L.S. Davey, *The Street Names of Lewes*, Lewes Town Council 1981
L.S. Davey, *The Inns of Lewes Past and Present*, Friends of Lewes 1977

Keystone, Ceres - Town Hall, High Street

In 1893 Samuel Denman of Brighton converted the Star Inn into the Town Hall with moulded red brick facade and keystones, including this one of Ceres, the Roman name for Demeter, the Greek goddess of agriculture and corn.

Keystone, Bacchus - Town Hall, High Street

The origins of the Town Hall, go back over 600 years. This is Bacchus, the God of Wine, one of five keenly cut and attractive keystones on the front of the building.

The Tourist Information Centre to the left, at the junction with Fisher Street, was once Albion Russell's shoe shop, the original home of Russell and Bromley shoes.

Terracotta leaf decoration - Market Tower, Market Street

Lewes market dates back to Saxon times. A wooden market house was built in the middle of the High Street, at the top of St Martin's Lane, about 1564. The present market tower was built in 1792 with funds from St Michael's Vestry. It houses the 16th century town bell, known as Gabriel, which originally came from St Nicholas Church, demolished in 1761. The terracotta decorations include a neat little design of ivy leaves and berries which also serve as air bricks.

3

Stone head of a man - Council Offices, Fisher Street

This carved 'grotesque' corbel stone is not the one which readers will see in position today. All four of the original 1913 'faces' carved by Perry Bridgeman were removed in 1996 because of vandalism and erosion from atmospheric pollution. In my opinion the modern copies are undersized and rather bland. The drawing shows the one head which survived and is at present in the safe keeping of Lewes District Council. The Friends of Lewes Civic Society has offered to share the costs of restoring this historical detail and making it ready for display in Lewes House on School Hill.

Plasterwork frieze - Council offices, Fisher Street

This rather fine mock-Tudor building was erected in 1913 for the borough council. The architect was Rowland H. Halls of Seveirg Chambers, Lewes, and the builders were Messrs Godfrey Bros.

The very attractive plasterwork decoration was carried out by G.P. Bankart of London. He took a long ten-mile walk over the South Downs with his sketch book to record the exact proportions of oxen and wagon. Look carefully at all the other pieces of plasterwork, including the lovely little floral designs on the side of the building.

Terracotta grotesque - 1 Market Lane

This amusing item was bought at the Amberley Chalk Pits Museum in about 1994. It depicts a satyr, a Greek god of the woodlands with long ears, represented by the Romans as part goat.

Hairdresser's hanging sign - Fisher Street

No words are needed to reinforce the simple message: the scissors and comb say it all. How much better this is than a garish illuminated box sign.

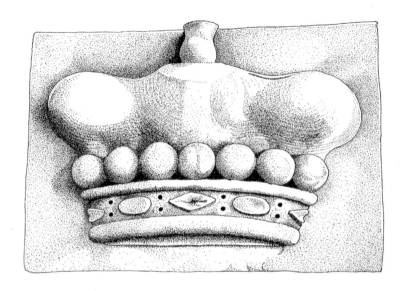

Stone coronet - Castle Precincts car park

On a low wall on the eastern side of the car park will be found a stone carving in relief of a viscount's coronet. Seven of the sixteen balls are shown.

Viscount is the 4th rank in the British peerage, the first creation being in 1440, but which local viscount this commemorates remains a mystery. A map of 1817 shows this area as gardens, although there may have been buildings here in earlier times as this piece of land falls within the original castle walls.

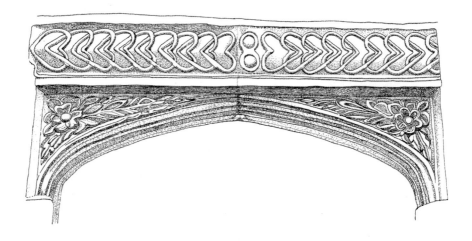

Tudor arch - Castle Ditch Lane

Lewes Castle moat was always dry, and Castle Ditch Lane now follows its course. It is approached from Popes Passage, next to the Rainbow Tavern, or via Fisher Street. At the foot of a flight of stone steps is a grade 2 listed building, an 18th century warehouse which incorporates a shallow Tudor archway.

This hidden treasure of Lewes is sadly neglected and very vulnerable to damage from traffic in this narrow cul-de-sac. Note the delicate pattern of interlocking hearts across the top.

Clock at Wallis & Wallis, auctioneers - West Street

The architect who designed this building for the Lewes Cooperative Society in 1905 seems to have been influenced by the Arts & Crafts style. During World War II a bomb dropped opposite, damaging what was New Street (1815), and it is said that the clock stopped at that moment. It has recently been restored to working order by Roy Butler, owner of Wallis & Wallis. Plans are in hand to restore the central spire above the clock face.

Horse and rider weathervane - North Street/Little East Street

A modern block of flats forms the corner of this Lewes District Council £750,000 housing project for the elderly, completed in the late 1970s. The architect Paul Hodgkin designed both the buildings and the weathervane, which depicts the Duke of Wellington on his black charger. The ironwork was produced by Ben Stevens at his Fisher Street forge in 1979. Nearby are Waterloo Place and Wellington Street.

Eastgate Stoneworks - opposite the bus station

Eastgate Stoneworks was established before 1727 by Arthur Morris. A back extension was built in 1907, with the Art Nouveau inscription *Established over a Century* low down on the wall beside the window. The company name, carved in stone, is supported at both ends by a snail-like spiral enclosing a flower and stems in a fashionable whiplash design.

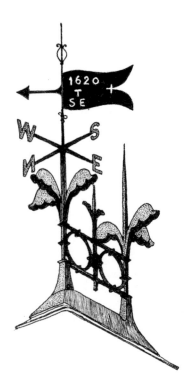

Weathervane at Harvey's Brewery - Bridge Wharf

The 19th century in Lewes was a flourishing time for brewing, and by 1823 the town had five breweries. Harvey & Son was founded in 1790, and in 1880 the original Georgian brewery was rebuilt by William Bradford with a handsome tower.

The weathervane, with a gilded pennon, the date 1620 and the initials TSE, was originally on the tower of St Thomas à Becket in the Cliffe. The vane was sold in 1751 for 4s 2d (21p), after which it disappeared for 129 years. Newly discovered, it was incorporated in the ironwork which decorates the top of the malthouse.

Tower on the Riverside Centre - Railway Lane

An attractive ventilation tower sits atop this building, which was erected in 1900 to house the Sunday school of the Tabernacle Congregational Chapel, demolished in 1955.

Forfars Bakers - corner of Railway Lane/Cliffe Bridge

This attractive wrought-iron wall bracket featuring a spiral ear of corn is probably modern, but it is a good choice to embellish the one remaining original building on this side of the shopping arcade.

Clock tower - Fitzroy House, Friars Walk

In 1862 the Fitzroy Memorial Library was built at Eastgate Corner. It was designed by Sir George Gilbert Scott in assured Venetian Gothic style, and funded by Baron Nathan Rothschild's daughter, the widow of Henry Fitzroy (1807-59), MP for Lewes. The elegant clock flêche (a slender spire) has survived in beautiful condition.

Much of this important building was restored in 1975 by James Franks and family, who are practical and enthusiastic campaigners for the preservation of all that is best in Lewes.

ESTABLISHED 1870

Lewes Building Society plaque at NatWest Bank - Friars Walk

This building (11 School Hill) was constructed about 1830 of buff-yellow bricks to balance a stuccoed base below. In 1853 it became the Lewes Dispensary and Infirmary premises. The Lewes Building Society set up business here in 1870, and was eventually taken over by the Southdown Building Society - which was, in turn, absorbed into the Leeds, and finally became the Halifax.

The design of the stone plaque features a mock-Tudor style house securely protected by a sturdy belt.

Bootscraper - 23 High Street (School Hill)

There are many cast-iron bootscrapers in Lewes, but this is a splendid and unusual one. Crested, 'starred' and supported by four strong lion's paws, it is almost too fine to be subjected to the muddy boot.

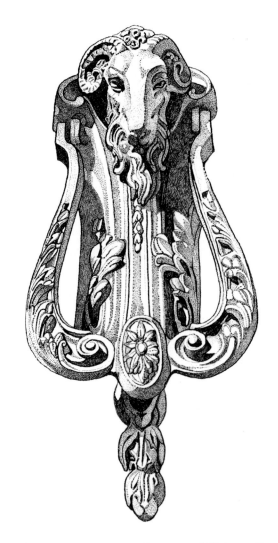

Doorknocker - Regency House, Albion Street

Regency House was built circa 1822. The architect was probably James Berry of Malling. The goat's head door-knocker looks modern, and has recently been carefully polished.

Iron vane and decoration - Lewes Library, Albion Street

On the corner of Albion Street and East Street is Lewes Library (1874), designed in Free Gothic as a School of Art by Henry Card, the county surveyor.

The two black iron banneret vanes were probably made in John Every's Phoenix Ironworks, situated on the west bank of the Ouse from 1835.

Stone archway - Friars Walk

A reset 15th century Perpendicular archway, perhaps from the Convent of Grey Friars which occupied an area between Friars Walk and the banks of the River Ouse.

Drinking fountain - Friars Walk

This drinking fountain was sited here in 1851, although the stone surround has the date 1874. It tapped the ancient Pinwell spring which bubbled up by the Friary wall opposite. In 1981 the wellhead was restored by the Friends of Lewes Civic Society.

Railway company crest - Lewes Station

The crest will be found on the wall to the left just beyond the booking hall. The plaque commemorates the building of Lewes's third station in 1888 by the London, Brighton & South Coast Railway (LBSCR).

The top left quarter represents the City of London and, reading clockwise, we see the Brighton dolphins, the star & crescent of Portsmouth and, finally, three 'demi-lions conjoined to three demi-ships' symbolising the Cinque Ports. The LBSCR was absorbed into the Southern Railway in 1923, into British Railways in 1948 and into Connex South Central in 1996.

The plaque was repainted in 1988. Unfortunately, some of the colours are incorrect.

Cast-iron girder - Lewes railway station

The present railway station, built in 1888 and brought into use the following year, replaced the 1857 station on an overlapping site which, in turn, replaced the original 1846 station in Friars Walk (on a site now partially occupied by the magistrates' court).

The Victorians believed that 'Ornament is the means by which Beauty is imparted to Utility', and certainly its application here has transformed this humble girder, silhouetted against the glass roof, into a work of art. The style is medieval, much favoured during the late Victorian period.

Wyvern roof finial - King's Head pub, Southover

This splendid roof finial was a standard product of the Keymer Brick and Tile Company's pottery, which used to be on Ditchling Common.

A wyvern differs from a dragon in that is has only two legs, and the wings are more bird-like. As a symbol it is possibly a cross between a Roman eagle and a Celtic dragon, reminding us of romanised Celts who offered resistance to invading Anglo-Saxons in the 5th century. It was adopted as a symbol by Alfred the Great of Wessex, who owned Ditchling, while the Bayeux Tapestry depicts a wyvern flag being carried in front of King Harold.

It happens that the wyvern was also the emblem of William de Warenne, and perhaps this accounts for its appearance on Lewes rooftops. There is another one on the roof of No. 5 North Way, off Nevill Green. You can see a similar wyvern roof finial at close quarters in Ditchling Museum.

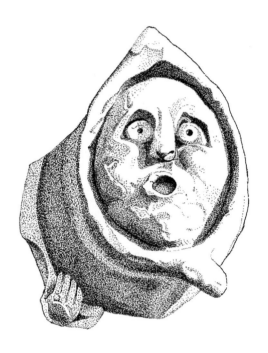

Monk's head - Grange Gardens, Southover

The archway and adjacent structures are made of Caen stone brought from the nearby St Pancras Priory, the great church of which was pulled down on the orders of Thomas Cromwell in 1538. It is by no means certain, however, that this carving of a monk's head dates from the Tudor period. The Grange was owned by John Gordon Woodhouse from 1901 until 1907. He was a keen landscape gardener and may have added it to the archway when making repairs and alterations.

His wife Violet was a celebrated harpsichord player, the first to make gramophone records of harpsichord music.

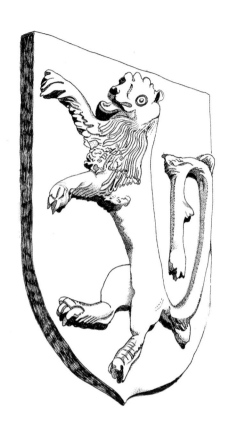

Newton coat of arms - The Grange, Southover High Street

The Grange was constructed in 1572 of Caen stone which was probably brought from the nearby St Pancras Priory, dissolved by Henry VIII in 1537. The builder of the Grange was William Newton, and the front of the building carries his coat of arms, a lion rampant.

Late in life he married John Evelyn's grandmother, then a widow, which is how the future diarist came to live in this house from 1630 to 1637.

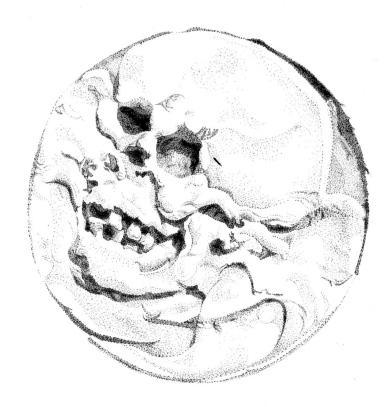

'Skull' gravestone - St John the Baptist, Southover

The details of this small carving of a skull will be apparent only in bright angled sunlight. The gravestone stands immediately inside the churchyard, on the left, against the boundary wall. The inscription, which is very worn, reads: 'Here lieth Mary, wife of Richard Mantell, who died on 22 December 1708.'

Richard, a market gardener, lived opposite, at the Red House in Southover High Street.

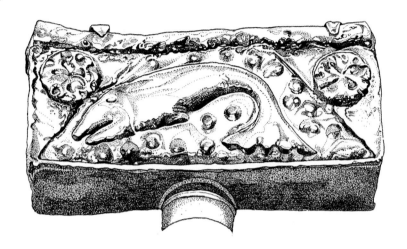

Rainwater hopper - Southover Manor

In Southover High Street, opposite Anne of Cleves Museum, stands Southover Manor, built for the brewer William Verral around 1840. On the boundary wall is this cast iron, or possibly painted lead, rainwater hopper featuring a leaping salmon. Note another hopper, with a bird design, close by.

The Swan Inn - Southover High Street/Bell Lane

The Swan Inn (circa 1770) began as The Bell. The beautiful leaded glass windows are perhaps late Victorian, and feature a mute swan surrounded by the exaggerated curving stems and buds typical of the Art Nouveau style.

Sun Insurance Company fireplate - Keere Street

Keere Street was so called as early as 1272, making it one of Lewes's oldest streets. Note the central watercourse paved with water-rolled flints or 'petrified kidneys', probably barged up from Newhaven beach. Tradition alleges that in the 13th century it was lined with the houses of Jewish merchants who were not allowed to live within the town walls.

The old Britannia Inn, No. 10, which was closed by the licensing authority in the 1920s, has a Sun Insurance Company lead fireplate attached to the wall. In heraldic terms the sun surrounded by rays is said to be 'in his splendour' and is usually depicted with a human face. Originally insurance companies had their own fire tenders and fighters, and would attend a fire only at those premises which displayed the correct fireplate and policy number.

Bootscraper - 4 Keere Street

This classical-style cast-iron bootscraper is in good condition. One doubts that it is used for the original purpose nowadays. A couple visiting from abroad asked me if it was designed to hold a milk bottle: a rather nice idea, I thought. Another of this design will be found in Mount Pleasant.

Terracotta plaque - Brewers Arms, High Street

In 1769 the brewer Obadiah Elliot bought the Ship Inn, where the churchwardens of St Michael's held their parish meetings. Renamed the Brewers Arms, it was sold on again in 1802 to the landlord James Wood.

The inn, which has medieval foundations, was popular with Chartists in the 1830s, and was rebuilt about the turn of the 20th century with mock-Tudor timbering and two very fine terracotta plaques. Both feature hops, grapes, oats and scroll work in high relief.

Leaf decoration - Freemasons Hall, High Street

In 1868 the Venetian Gothic style Freemasons Hall was adorned with Ruskinian foliage designs which are matched by the brackets of the immaculate drainpipes.

Ammonite capital - Castle Place, 166 High Street

Numbers 1-4 Castle Place were designed in circa 1815 by Amon Wilds, a Lewes builder-cum-architect, for Thomas Read Kemp. Around 1819 Wilds merged Nos 2 and 3 for the geologist Gideon Mantell, adding the Ionic porch and the giant pilasters with big scrolly fossil ammonites which certainly make excellent volutes.

Amon Wilds may have been attracted to what is sometimes called 'the ammonite order' by the coincidence of the pun on his Christian name.

Keystone - 167 High Street

This keystone of around 1814 is called 'The Laughing Boy' and is made of a product called Coade-stone - which is not stone at all, but a kind of terracotta. Certain clays and sands were mixed together according to a secret formula which is now lost. Coade-stone was used from the 1770s for over half a century, and has proved far more durable than most varieties of stone.

The architectural historian Sir Nikolaus Pevsner called this particular keystone 'a sweet little thing'.

Lion's head - Leo Cottage, New Road

This is a rather unusual lion's head, not the classic door-knocker kind.

The present owner of the early Victorian property applied for permission to make alterations to the front elevation. That was granted, but local officials voiced concern about the future of the lion, suggesting that the 'carving' was of historical importance. During renovation work it was discovered that 'Leo' is made of plaster but, despite his lack of antiquity, this particular lion is a delight.

Gothic-style window - 4A Paddock Terrace (White Hill)

This interesting and attractive Gothic-style window actually faces down Paddock Road, although it is part of the corner of Paddock Terrace. Perhaps the Art Nouveau leaded lights were added to 1870ish tracery.

Royal Mail box - Park Road

There are six Edward VII postboxes in Lewes. The crown-and-lettering cipher of this one is still reasonably crisp. Compare this good example with another at Star Corner, opposite the tourist information centre, which has been badly blurred by too many layers of paint.

The Lewes delivery office manager hopes to tap a special fund available for the renovation of such postboxes: the lettering is to be emphasised in gold.

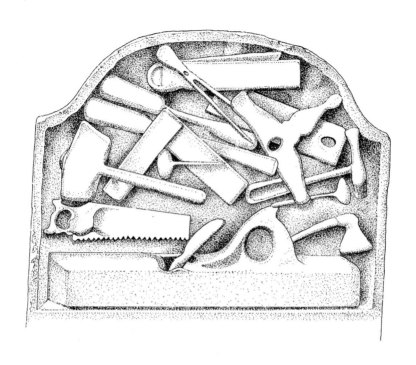

Footstone - St John sub Castro churchyard

The churchyard is approached via Lancaster Street and Church Row. The footstone to Mark Sharp (*MS 1747*), a carpenter, will be found off to the right, about halfway down the slope. At least thirteen different carpenter's tools have been carved, but they are fully discernible only in bright angled sunlight.

Note the dramatic Resurrection scene on Sharp's headstone.

Armorial emblems and motto at 16 Nevill Road

(not on map)

The estate of Lord Abergavenny owned the racecourse on the Downs further up the hill, and these three Victorian cottages (1899). The centre one is decorated with crisp terracotta emblems which carry the motto of the Most Noble Order of the Garter HONI SOIT QUI MAL Y PENSE *(Shame on him who thinks evil of it)*.

The order was instituted by King Edward III in 1348 and is the premier English order of chivalry. The same heraldic insignia will be found over the fireplace in the lounge of the White Hart Hotel, and also at St Peter's Place (1868), built for Lord Nevill, heir to Lord Abergavenny, where the punning motto is NE VILE VELIS *(Wish no evil)*.

41

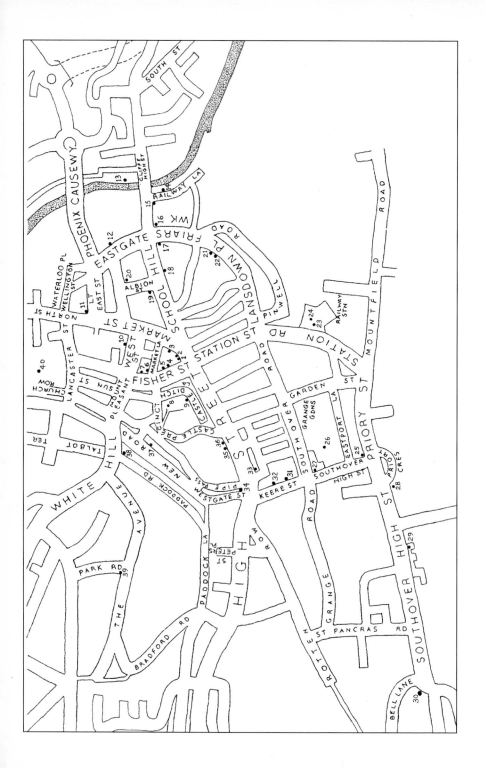

KEY TO MAP

The figures relate to the page numbers in the book

1 Keystone, Ceres - Town Hall, High Street
2 Keystone, Bacchus - Tow Hall, High Street
3 Terracotta leaf decoration - Market Tower
4 Stone head - Fisher Street
5 Plasterwork frieze - Fisher Street
6 Terracotta grotesque - Market Lane
7 Hairdresser's hanging sign - Fisher Street
8 Stone coronet - Castle Precinct car park
9 Tudor arch - Castle Ditch Lane
10 Auctioneers' clock - West Street
11 Weathervane - North Street/Little East Street
12 Eastgate Stoneworks - opp. bus station
13 Harvey's weathervane - Bridge Wharf
14 Ventilation tower - Riverside Centre
15 Forfars Bakers - 1 High Street (Cliffe)
16 Clock tower, Fitzroy House - High Street
17 Building society plaque - Friars Walk
18 Bootscraper - 23 High Street (School Hill)

19 Door knocker - Regency House, Albion Street
20 Iron vane and decoration - Albion Street
21 Stone archway - Friars Walk
22 Drinking fountain - Friars Walk
23 Railway company crest - Lewes station
24 Cast-iron girder - Lewes railway station
25 Wyvern roof finial - Kings Head, Southover
26 Monk's head - Grange Gardens, Southover
27 Newton coat of arms - The Grange, Southover
28 Skull gravestone - St. John Baptist, Southover
29 Rainwater hopper - Southover Manor
30 The Swan Inn - Southover High St/Bell Lane
31 Sun Insurance Co. fireplate - Keere Street
32 Bootscraper - 4 Keere Street
33 Terracotta plaque - Brewers Arms, High St.
34 Leaf decoration - Freemasons Hall, High St.
35 Ammonite capital - Castle Place, 166 High St.
36 Keystone - 167 High Street
37 Lion's head - Leo Cottage, New Road
38 Gothic style window - 4A Paddock Terrace
39 Royal Mail postbox - Park Road
40 Carpenter's footstone - St. John sub Castro

INDEX

44